How To Land The Job You Want

By: Jennifer Santiago Benson

HOW TO LAND THE JOB YOU WANT

BY: JENNIFER SANTIAGO BENSON

"Aspiring to Success is all a frame of thinking. Landing the job you want is an expression of thought."

Jennifer Santiago Benson

Dedication:

This book is dedicated to my father, who taught me that hard work and dedication will reap a bounty of success. Thank you, daddy, I love you.

Chapter 1:
How to find the job you are looking for

In these difficult economic times it may seem harder and harder for the average person to get a job. The fact that you purchased this book today tells me that you may fall into this category or perhaps you are simply looking to change careers. Whatever your motivation for buying this book may be, I am here to tell you that you have made a wise investment in yourself.

Over the next few chapters I am going to go into some detail about how to look for, apply for, and interview for the job you want.

The reality is that times have changed, and with these changing times, the roles of the job seeker have changed. What does that mean for you? It means that if you are going to survive you will have to make some changes as well.

But don't fret; the great thing about change is that some change can be good. It may not always seem good at the time or even comfortable for that matter, but ultimately change can and usually is a good thing.

Changing your thinking to make you more profitable to employers is the same thing that will one day allow you to own and operate your own business if you so desire.

As you may know, these past few years there has been a shift in the economy.

You or someone you know may have been directly affected by this shift. Sadly, many families are losing their homes and their jobs. It is when things seem darkest that you are able to see the light.

This chapter is going to focus first on deciding what job you want and how to look for it. Let me tell you that it is very easy to get wrapped up in the Internet job search and while this search method has helped countless people find great jobs it has also made it harder to make yourself stand out from the competition.

Let me put it to you this way, do you think that "Bob" the local grocery store owner is going to be more likely to hire "Jane" who applied online or "You" who went into the store and had a face to face conversation with "Bob" where you were able to discuss with him why you are the right person for the job.

Now I know what you must be thinking, if Bob were hiring in my town the position would already be filled before I even got up in the morning. That may be so in this case, you have to now ask yourself why you didn't get up earlier.

Now let's get back to the basics. When you are trying to decide what type of job you are looking for you have to sit down and think about your strengths as a person. Everyone has something that they are good at. What are you good at?

As an employer and hiring manager, I have interviewed many different people. One of the main reasons I would discard an application or not hire a person after an interview is if I discover that the person in front of me is not really interested in the position I am offering. I ask myself 'If they didn't want to do this type of work, why did they interview here?' Don't get me wrong, I understand that at this point you may be thinking you just want a job so you can be gainfully employed but this may not be the right mindset.

You will get a job much faster when you are going after something that you either, A. Have a passion about, or B. You are good at.

That is it! It is really that simple. So, right now, the first thing you need to do is write down a few things you think you are good at.

Are you a good swimmer? (You could possibly be a life-guard, camp instructor, swim coach, etc.) Can you charm a person when you talk to them? (Maybe you could work in a business office, front desk, sales, car salesmen, etc.) Do you know your cars? (You could consider being a mechanic, auto-body specialist, professional detailer, etc.) Are you starting to see what I am saying?

The very first step to finding the job you are looking for is to know what you want to do. Once you have it narrowed down you can focus your efforts on developing your resume to target the career you have selected.

If you have chosen more than one that is OK. You would just want to create more than one resume. Each resume should be unique for the job you are applying to. Trust me; you will stand out with a well written and well thought out resume.

One of the things to keep in mind when creating a killer resume is to keep it clear, concise, and no more than 2 pages. The reason why you do not want it to be longer than 2 pages is because sometimes too much work history can be just as cancerous as too little work history. Think about it from the employer's point of view. If you had 2 candidates to choose from, the first candidate has been with the same company for 15 years but this company had to downsize or closed their doors due to the poor economy. The second candidate has had a different job every few months and has done many different types of jobs during the course of that same 15 year span. Which one would you want to hire?

If you are the person with the "colorful" resume don't fret. I am the Queen of colorful resumes; I have used the technique that I am telling you about right now to be very successful in spite of it. Working my resume so that each job showed closely related to the job I was applying for.

If I wanted to be a cashier, I would focus on my resume on describing the positions where I handled cash. Perhaps you are in need of an example.

Let's say for example I worked at Store A as a cashier.
Store B: I was a sales associate who occasionally handled cash

Store C: I was a supervisor who managed a team of cashiers
Store D: I was a waitress
Store E: I provided telephone support and occasionally took payments.

Here is how I would attempt to word it. (Please do keep in mind that this is not an example of a resume only an example of wording)

Store A: Handled company funds daily. Registers balanced properly daily.
Store C: Supervised team of cashiers to ensure proper handling of funds. Registers balanced properly daily.
Store D: Assisted customers with their orders as well as handled payments.

Are you starting to see how it is done? There are many resume writing workshops and companies. If you are just getting started though you can use one of Microsoft Word Templates to help you get started. If you know someone who has experience with writing resumes you might also see if they could lend some assistance or offer feedback on what you have written. A well written resume will get seen most of the time.

Here is a resume template. The more experience you have the longer the resume will be.

First Name, Last Name
Address, City, State, Zip
Contact Number
Email Address

Job Title
Objective: This is the section used to describe in summary both what you are looking for as well as what you will bring to the position if selected.

Area of
Expertise

This section is used to identify your strengths. If you are new to the job market do not add this section.

Professional
Experience

Use this section to document your previous work history. If none, you will replace this section with volunteer activities and/or any school accomplishments that are in-line with the position you are seeking.

Education and
Certifications

This section is where you will document our education, awards, certifications, licenses, etc.

Now that you know how to decide what type of job you want, and you have your resume ready to go, it is time to start your job search.

Believe it or not, the first place to look for a job is in the newspaper, if, you do not have a computer. I would recommend going to your local internet cafe or your community center, or even your local unemployment office as an alternative as well. The unemployment office should have a computer available for use for those who are actively seeking employment.

Some offices may even have job postings in their office. This is the perfect place to get started especially if you have been out of work for a while.

So, now you have your resume and you know what you want to do. One thing and I cannot stress this enough, if you join one of the online job sites, DO NOT AUTO submit resumes. While this is the easiest thing to do the chances of your resume being seen are very slim.

Some people would recommend you choose to use auto submit. If you do use this method it will be harder for you to put the rest of this book to good use because this book was designed with the understanding that the position you are applying for you want and have thoroughly researched.

However, if you are auto submitting to positions that are in line with what you are looking for, you can still use these techniques. While it is not recommended you have to do what works best for you. This is after all, your future we are talking about.

Whatever you decide though, you will be successful in finding the job you want because knowing what you want to do is half the battle.

Chapter 2:
The Cover Letter

When you are trying to get a job that requires a cover letter, having a well written and well thought out cover letter will separate you from the competition.

One of the things to keep in mind when creating your cover letter is you will want to know the company you are applying to. Doing your research on the company you are submitting your resume to will help you develop a great cover letter.

Think about the cover letter like this, if I asked you to tell me why I should hire you what would you say?

The cover letter is a chance to briefly sell yourself as an individual, to the potential employer. A poorly written cover letter means your resume has a slim chance of being seen. If your resume does not get seen you don't get the job.

Here are a few things to take into consideration when writing a cover letter.

Know your target. If you happen to know

who the hiring manager is, direct the cover letter to that person. For example if you know the person reviewing the resume is named Jane Smith. You would want to address the letter to Jane Smith and not to the Hiring Manager.

To put it in simpler terms a cover letter is a personal letter to the person who is going through the resumes. In some companies a computer is the first point of contact for resumes and covers letters. When you are face to face with a computer making sure your resume is written for the company, and position you are applying to, is going to work well with the computer.

The next thing you need to know when writing a good cover letter:

Keep it concise. It is tempting to try to do the interview on the cover letter but that is not always the best way. Many times the potential employer is scouring through hundreds or even thousands of applications. If your cover letter is too long it won't get read. If they don't read the cover letter, they are not going to read the resume.

Here is a sample cover letter.

Today's Date

Dear Hiring Manager:

My name is YOUR NAME HERE. I saw your position at (PLACE WHERE YOU SAW POSITION) and I am very interested in this position.

In my previous employment I was (DESCRIBE PREVIOUS EMPLOYMENT TO INCLUDE BASIC RESPONSIBILITIES)

I have experience in (THIS LINE IS USED TO SELL YOURSELF, WHAT MAKES YOU UNIQUE, WHAT MAKES ME WANT TO LOOK AT YOUR RESUME)EX: client services, sales, property management, cost control, and building maintenance.

(THIS IS YOUR CLOSING STATEMENT) EX: I am confident in my customer service skills and my management skills would be an asset in this role.

Thank you for your time and consideration. I hope to have the opportunity to discuss the opening with you in person.

Thank you for your considerations. I have included my resume for your review.

YOU NAME HERE
YOUR CONTACT NUMBER
YOUR EMAIL ADDRESS

Just keep this in mind. Economic times are not what they used to be and employers can be picky when it comes to selecting the perfect person for the job. They don't have to read your cover letter if it looks too long or even read your resume if it goes on and on for days. The employer already has a general idea of what they are looking for. They are looking for you; they just don't realize it yet.

Your cover letter is an expression of who you are and what you have to offer. If you are a college graduate, mentioning that along with some of your accomplishments in school would be a good way to let the employer know right from the start a little bit about you.

If you are not a college graduate you will want to stay away from talking about your education. Too little education may eliminate you before you even get your foot in the door. The secret around this, don't mention your education in your cover letter. Mention your strengths and what you can bring to the position.

Try to answer the question: Why should I hire you? (You will want to do this before you ever go in for an interview.)

Last thing you should do when writing an effective cover letter:

Focus. A well thought out, focused, and concise cover letter will be read more often than not.

An important thing to keep in mind though when you are looking for a job is if you are trying to get a job in which you have no experience and no education, you will run into several road blocks. Does this mean you won't or can't get the job? No. One of the things I have learned over the years is it is all about presentation, Presentation, and Presentation.

Unless you are applying for a commission based sales position, too much arrogance can have the potential employer putting your resume in the "Do Not Call" pile.

Now you have the basics down on writing a cover letter. You may be wondering what if you have never written a cover letter before. Do you still need one?

Honestly, not every job that is hiring is going to be looking for, need, or require a cover letter.

Most companies would like a resume. However,
There are exceptions to every rule.

If you end up not needing a cover letter or a resume, I can tell you one thing. It would not hurt you to have one prepared.

Also, a good thing to keep on your person especially if you are doing door to door applications is a folder. Have in your folder several copies of your resume and a separate list of references.

References are desired in each and every position I have ever seen, applied to, or talked to others about.

Now there may be companies that do not check references but most will require them and reserve the right to contact them.

Having a list of references handy can be incredibly helpful to you in your career search.

If you are planning on driving around to see what is available, and you happen to notice a help wanted sign. Having a resume and list of references can be helpful to you for when you fill out those applications on the spot.

With this method, you can pull out your resume and references and just copy it onto the company application. Some companies even have on the spot interviews so if you are going to stop in to pick up an application try to dress to impress. No one will expect you to be in a business suit, but it would not hurt to look clean cut and well-kept when walking through the door.

I digress; just remember that a cover letter is a reflection of who you are. You can also find templates online to help give you an idea of where to start but please don't just copy and paste the template. Make it your own. Create a picture of yourself that the employer can see.

You will stand out with a well written resume. It tells the employer that you care about their company and the position that is available.

Chapter 3:
It is all about the mindset

One of the things I have experienced during my many interviews over the years is an expectant mindset makes the difference between a good interview and a bad interview.

Let me give you an example. I discovered this employment opportunity while doing my daily job search. I did some research on the company, and I created my resume and cover letter to match what they were looking for. When I was called about an interview I had a few minutes to speak with the person who I would be meeting with. During this conversation I instantly knew that I would not be happy working for this company and that the interview was not going to go well.

Pushing aside those thoughts I proceeded to prepare for my interview. I will go into the preparation process in a later chapter. The day of my interview, I was dressed to impress and ready to go. I arrived at my destination early since it was further then I had wanted to travel I did not do a dry run to the location.

While I waited, I watched, I watched the company, the employees, and the customers. I like to do that sometimes because I believe you can get a good feeling for the environment you will be working. You can tell a lot about a place by the employees.

It was at this point I began to have that same uneasy feeling. I started feeling more and more like this was not right and it was not going to work out.

By the time it was time for my interview my blood pressure had raised, I was sweating, and feeling completely unraveled. Well, naturally, I thought due to my history and experience I could bounce back from this but during the interview I could sense that it was all going wrong.

When the interviewer did not shake my hand, I knew right there that I did not have the position. It had been solidified for me. There were other signals during the interview that told me that I did not get it.

One way to know whether or not you impress your interviewer is if the interviewer is throwing things at you even when your responses are perfect, chances are they do not think you are a right fit. I will use this interview as an example.

When I was asked if I was comfortable selling on the phone, my response was "yes of course" and I followed that with some examples of my experiences on the phone. The interviewer's response to my statement was "Well, it sounds to me like you are used to instant gratification sales, we are more of a building value sales organization." Did you see that? While, my response had been an impressive response that had worked several times before, this interviewer was not interested.

Some could argue that this interviewer was looking for someone with a different skill set. Well, think about this. I was selected for the interview because of my resume and cover letter. Both of these items describe my skill set. Make sense?

To be quite frank with you, I didn't get the job because I didn't want the job. I knew walking into the office that I was making a mistake being there, and even though the words coming out of my mouth were impressive, my actions and my body language were screaming ,"Get Me OUTTA Here!"

When you have a positive mindset (you go into the interview expecting the job) and a positive expectation for your interview (you already know that the interviewer is going to love you) you have already overcome half of the battle. This is a visualization exercise; the theory behind this exercise is that what goes on deep inside your subconscious is the same thing that is going on in your physical world.

If you want the job and you believe you would be great at that job, you need to truly believe that there is not going to be one person walking through that door that will be better than you. You are the person that this interviewer is looking for. If you believe that both inside and out when you walk into that interview you will walk into that interview in such a way that the interviewer will have no choice but to seriously consider you as a candidate.

In fact, depending on the company and the hiring policy, you may even walk out of the interview with the job, or at worst a second interview.

Here is the thing to keep in mind in case you are saying to yourself that what I am saying sounds crazy. Just think about this for a moment. Have you ever had a moment when you felt so confident about something, you just knew it deep within your being that it was going to be so and it was? Maybe, you studied for a test and felt so good about it. The day you tested, everything looked familiar and after the test you felt great. When you received your test results you got the score you knew you were going to get?

Let's look at it in reverse now. You took a test, you did not feel confident about, and you felt nervous and had a sick feeling in the pit of your stomach that kept aching telling you that you did not pass the test. When you got the results you discover to no surprise that you failed?

That feeling, that inner voice is called many things too many different people. This inner voice though, knows the answers already. When you really listen to it, you will hear it. Don't mistake the voices of family and friends for your inner voice. If someone is telling you that the economy is bad and there is no work, DO NOT BELIEVE THEM. There is work.

I tested that theory this year. I was given 4 concrete; you can start tomorrow offers that

I turned down. I was called and invited to interview 3 times, which I politely declined, and I was emailed at least a dozen more times with requests to submit a formal application. My point is, there is work, and there are jobs. Never let anyone tell you what you can and cannot do. You are the maker of your own destiny.

You do not have to settle either, get that thought out of your mind right now. I was offered for one of those 4 positions a significantly lower pay then I was accustomed to. I declined the offer telling them that it was unacceptable to me. I received a counter offer which was significantly more than the original offer. The point I am trying to make here is that I determined my worth and value and I expressed my worth to the potential employer in such a way that the employer discovered the value as well as offered me what I believed I was worth.

The first thing you have to do is decide what job you want. Once you have decided on that, decide what you want to be paid. Keep in mind that fixed rate companies might not be flexible with their offer. A fixed rate company has a standard offer that is not negotiable, for example all new employees start at $9 per hour. You don't want to go into that interview and demand $12. That is the part I mentioned about doing your research on the company. You need to know the hiring trends, employee to employer relationship, and if possible any benefits that the company may offer BEFORE you go into the interview.

The times have changed, and as you know the economy is not where it used to be. Employers do have a choice and they are looking for someone that can provide them with value for the money. In today's market, you really don't want to walk in asking about compensation and benefits packages. You should already have a good idea about these features and when asked by the interviewer if you have any questions, you could mention some of the information you know about the company and follow it with a question you have in relation to something you have already read and know about.

Let me give you an example. The interviewer asks you "Do you have any questions for me?" you can respond by saying something like "Well actually, I was reading your company website and it was discussing the great culture, benefits packages, and the fact that you recently entered into the fortune 1000. That is very impressive. I am wondering how advancement works, I can see myself moving very far in this company."

Do you see what I did there? I asked a question but only after showing the interviewer that I know that I am talking about. I know this company, and not only that. I know I am already getting the job because I talked about advancement and seeing myself moving very far. Most interviewers are not looking for temporary employees they are looking for good people that are going to stay with them for a long time. Why is this? Simple, it costs money to train a new employee and process the paperwork. It cost a company less time and money to keep an employee as long as possible.

Having confidence and the expectation that the job you are applying for is already yours are great steps in the right direction.

Wanting the job is not enough, you have to believe you are going to get the job. If you don't believe, you will find it very difficult to attain.

Chapter 4: The Pre-Interview

Over the past few chapters we talked about deciding what type of work you are looking for, creating a resume and cover letter to match the job you want and developing a winner's mentality - having a belief in yourself that you are going to get the job.

You have done all the work, submitted your resume, called prospective employers and scheduled interviews. You now have your first interview and you need to know what to do to prepare for it.

First things first, remember how in the beginning I talked about doing your homework on the company you are interested in working for? Preliminary Interviews are the best time to get focused and get studying.

A few things to check out on the company you are interested in:

First, you want to see how long the company has been in business. How long they have been in business is a good conversation item and is also helpful for you to know.

If the company has a website online review it beforehand. Read the "About" section. Take it all in.

Write down items you find interesting or have questions about. You could use this information when the interviewer asks you if you have any questions for them.

Knowing the pay range or pay rate before you go into the interview is also a good idea. There are several reasons why having this information available to you before you go into the interview. Depending on where you are at in your life, or depending on your work experience, you may be asked by the interviewer what your salary expectations are.

This is used during the interview process for several reasons but what it means for you is that if hired, the salary you indicated during the interview is what you are most likely to get.

Of course, there are exceptions to every rule as each company determines pay differently but the purpose of this book is to try to prepare you for most positions.

There are many positions and job listings that will have the salary listed. In this case they have done that part of the research for you.

If they have not, it would be a good idea to sit down and decide on what would be a reasonable amount of money for your time before applying. Look at your past work history as a guide to help you place a fair market value on your services.

You may be thinking "I was in college during my last job, making $8 an hour. Now I have a degree and should make much more! How much more should I ask for?"

That is a good question and to be honest it really depends on the type of degree you have, the school you went to, etc. All of these are factors when deciding what your starting pay rate should be. My best advice to you would be to do some research at your university so that you can have a better understanding of the starting pay scale for your career field. This can help you be better armed and prepared when you graduate from the university.

Your pay usually will be determined by the industry standard for your line of work.

An engineer is going to earn a different starting salary from a nurse, or a massage

therapist for example can earn a fair living, in some cases a very comfortable living depending again on past experiences, client satisfaction, and return customers. Starting out though, their pay would be fairly low.

Are you starting the see the picture I am trying to paint for you?

Doing your research is always the best way to ensure you can ask for a fair rate of pay during your interview.

My main goal and focus for you is to give you a solid foundation so that when you do interview you are prepared, and informed. That you have a good and clear understanding on what they are looking for so that you can walk into the interview as the expert the company is seeking.

The reality is the economy is getting better. It is happening slowly and maybe in your town it is still not where it needs to be. I understand but I don't want you to put this book down and say it doesn't apply to you because no one is hiring.

You have to look at it as no one you "know" is hiring. Broaden your search radius, and broaden your overall search.

So, by now you have a good idea of the amount of money you would like to receive for the position you are applying to. You may be asking yourself why you need to figure this out now, why can't you go in and just ask them what they are paying.

Well, that brings me again to my previous statement about different company cultures. Some companies do not wish to disclose this information. Rather, they want you to come into the interview prepared with an annual/Monthly/Weekly/Hourly rate already in mind.

This helps the potential employer in many ways, the main way and the one I will share with you today is money. If I have two candidates to choose from that are equal to me in every way except monetarily, I am going to go with the one who is going to cost me less to hire. Will I do this always? Will the person you are going to interview with do this always? Not necessarily, if your skills and personality are of great worth to the interviewer they will look past the higher salary and choose to hire you.

It all boils down to the impression you make during the interview which is why preparing for the interview is one of the most important things you can do.

So now you know what the pay scale is and if not, you have a general idea of what you would like to be paid. It is a good idea to do a search to see the average pay scale for that position in your area, this way you could keep your salary requirements as close to the average as possible.

You can find this information at www.indeed.com/salary

Next thing you want to do is make sure you have an updated resume, cover letter, and list of references. Having a list of references readily available can prove very valuable to you during the interview process. Some companies have internal applications that they need you to fill out when you arrive at your interview. Having the resume and references available for quick and easy reference will make completing the application very easy for you.

Making things easier for you is very

important because the less stress prior to the interview, the better the interview. You will be under less stress if you are well prepared.

When you are running down your pre-interview checklist you will want to be sure that you don't forget the outfit.

Have you ever heard the saying "you are what you wear"? This is very true when it comes to interviews. You are judged almost instantly by what you choose to wear for an interview.

This is why I mentioned to you before about doing a dry run. What this means is that whenever possible visit the location before your interview. You don't have to tell them that is why you are there; you just want to casually see what the dress code is by observing the employees.

If they are dressed in business casual for work, you will want to at a minimum dress in business casual for the interview. If they are wearing business professional, you will want to wear business professional. If they are wearing uniforms, you could get away with wearing business casual. If you are a male a suit is usually a good idea. However, if you are going to be interviewing for a construction job you will want to avoid wearing a suit. The key to a successful interview is to impress the interviewer. For this type of interview you might want to consider wearing a nice button down shirt and jeans (possibly slacks,) this would be acceptable in many cases.

At the end of the day, the general idea behind what to wear for an interview would be to focus on the things that should never be worn to an interview. Never wear clothing with holes in it. Never wear shorts and a tee-shirt unless you are trying to be a life-guard. Flip-flops are usually a no-no, so avoid them whenever possible.

I almost forgot to mention, you should always be presentable including your hair, so make sure all of you looks great.

Ladies, avoid the miniskirts they are great for going out but not great for interviews. Skirts are acceptable but keep them from being too short. You never know who is going to be interviewing you and sometimes too short can mean "Next!" if you get my meaning.

And please, don't bring pets, children, boyfriends, girlfriends, mothers, best-friends, etc. to your job interview. If they must come, have them wait outside. Bringing others with you to the interview tells the interviewer that you lack the confidence to come alone. It is also a red-flag that you might bring them with you to work often. This can be a turn-off and you may find yourself walking out without a job.

There was this one time, I was interviewing for an assistant manager position at one of my properties when one of my interviewees arrived to her interview with her dog in her bag. I was surprised, this was the first time that had ever happened to me. When she walked around the counter I noticed her short shorts, and flips-flops. I couldn't believe it! There was a sign on the front door that clearly stated no pets allowed except for seeing eye dogs and here she was, coming to interview for a management position with her pet. First impressions can be lasting ones.

Overall, the most important thing to remember when getting ready for the big interview is this: When you are prepared, you are confident.

Charm goes a long way but it starts with being prepared, knowing what you want, knowing about the company, knowing what you would like to earn, and knowing what you are going to wear.

As I mentioned earlier, it is all about presentation. (Having the skill set doesn't hurt either)

Chapter 5: The Interview

By this point you should be really proud of yourself. You have gotten this far and believe me when I say that getting an interview is a huge step in the right direction.

Congratulations!

You have refined your resume, cover letter, appearance, and presentation. You are ready for the big day.

When going to the interview it is standard to arrive 15 minutes early unless noted otherwise.

Before you head out don't forget to make sure you have a few copies of your resume, list of references and a cover letter. The cover letter is not mandatory but it will separate you from most everyone else.

This cover letter will be prepared a bit differently because it is now focused on the interviewing manager and assumes you have already been offered an interview. This cover letter will highlight your strengths and reinforce to the interviewer why you are the perfect person for the position.

When you are called into the interview a firm handshake will send a positive message, a handshake however that is overly aggressive will off-putting. If you are unsure, test your handshake on both males and females to be sure that it is firm but not over powering. A handshake is a reflection of who you are, so it is important to try to keep it sincere. Don't try to fake it. Just be confident in yourself and it will show in your handshake.

When asked to sit down you will want to take the seat closer to the interviewer and make sure that you are sitting well composed. Do not slouch. Never slouch. Sit tall. Tall equals pride in yourself, in your appearance and in what you can bring to the table. A slouch denotes fear, insecurity, lack of confidence, and ultimately, that you might not be the person they are looking for.

The way you sit is important for almost any type of job you are applying to. Your posture says a lot to the potential employer. A deep slouch gives off the image that you are not really interested in this job offer and that if selected you will not really care about it.

Consider this for a moment, you are sitting in a restaurant and you see a couple sitting across from you. The couple appears to be arguing but one of the partners is slouched into the chair while the other partner is upright and noticeably speaking. What would be your first thought?

The truth of the matter is that an interview is a chance to get a feel for the type of person you are. A face to face interview can show a lot to the potential employer that the interviewee may not even realize that they are showing.

Next thing to avoid is fidgeting. This can be very challenging especially if you are prone to being nervous during an interview. If you feel these urges wrap your figures together and place them on your lap. This will assist you in keeping the nerves at bay and your body from taking over. I have done this a few times especially for important interviews and when my nerves where on end. It helped me to get centered and refocus. Once the nerves went away I would release my hands.

Please don't sit on your hands though. That does not look professional.

Now that you are comfortable the interviewer is going to ask you a series of questions. Depending on the type of job, skill set they are seeking, and other factors these questions can range from simple to difficult.

It is best to have mentally prepared several answers to common questions.

Some common questions would be:

Why are you interested in this position?
Tell me a little bit about yourself?
Where do you see yourself in 5, 10 years?
What are your salary requirements?
What would a previous employer say about you if they were contacted?

Please keep in mind that these are common questions but not every employer will use these questions. Some of even none of these may be asked. The best way to be prepared in all honesty is to know your potential employer and know yourself.

You know who you are and you know what makes you special. If you know about the company you are ahead of the game because most of the questions you will be asked will have to do or be based around those two things.

Don't stress over the actual interview. In fact, the best way to be successful during the interview is to do all of your stressing beforehand. What I mean is checking, double checking, triple checking everything to make sure you are as prepared as you can possibly be. This way you free up your mind during the interview to talk about you and what makes you special.

It all boils down to preparation, mentality, appearance, and preparation. Yes, I know I wrote preparation twice, it was to emphasize how important it is to be prepared.

There are a few things that you should NOT do during an interview. When you are interviewing here are a few tips of items that are best left off the table of discussion:

Never bad mouth a previous employer, it sends a very negative message to the interviewer and may possibly cost you the position. I want you to put yourself in the interviewer's position for just a moment, would you want to be friends with someone who talks about other people behind their back? Not really? Why? It is because you could never really trust this person. You can never know whether or not they will one day tell someone else terrible things about you.

This is how bad mouthing a previous employer is like. If you are saying all of these terrible things, even if you believe they are true, it is going to make you look bad.

No one wants to bring someone on board who can turn around and make their company look bad. It is just bad business. As an interviewer how do I know that you won't get angry one day, quit, and tell all your friends about how terrible my company was?

Especially, in a time where communication is at an all-time high and everyone knows everything about everything. A negative employee is simply not desirable.

Leave the negativity at the door. If you didn't have a good experience at the previous job don't dwell on the negative experience, discuss what you learned from the experience. And move on. You now have an even better understanding of what you are looking for in a company.

Find a way to turn the negative into a position. Find a way to use the bad experience to your advantage. These are also something's that you can do in the pre-interview phase if needed.

Finally, allow the interviewer to speak and ask questions but try not to let the interviewer do all of the talking. The interview time is a chance for you to shine. Talk, tell your story. When the interviewer is ready to move on to the next question they will tell you. Allow the interviewer room to move the interview forward, but try not to leave too much dead air between topics.

During an interview, you should do most of the talking. Otherwise, you are not using the time efficiently. If they insist on doing most of the talking, that means they aren't interested in what you have to say. That means you aren't doing a good job selling yourself. The goal is to actively engage your interviewer. They should be actively listening to your stories and picturing you in the role you are applying for.

When the interviewer is doing all the talking, that means that they are not thinking about what you have said. You have not sold yourself. They are working, not you. Focus, breathe, and sell yourself but know when to stop talking.

If you are interrupted, stop talking and listen. When an opportunity opens up, resume selling yourself.

Remember this interview is about you.

You are there because the company saw something in you that they found interesting enough to invite you to interview.

That is a great thing.

When your interview is over, you will have either a good feeling or a bad one. If you have a good feeling WONDERFUL! Give yourself a pat on the back for a job well done.

If you have a bad feeling, don't fret. Go back to the basics and try again. Keep pressing forward. When they call you back, you can start your new job and know that you made it happen.

You have the power within you to do great things and find that job you have been looking for. You have done it, you have gone through the interview and you are still standing.

In the next chapter I will briefly talk about something's you might want to do after the interview. These are not required but can go a long way in helping you to stand out.

Breathe in, breathe out, relax, the challenging part is over.

Chapter 6: The Post-Interview

Now, you have done the interview and you are waiting to hear back from the employer. A good way to stand out from the competition would be to send a nice thank you note.

In this chapter I will review a few things and briefly touch on some newer hiring methods that are being used by employers.

As I mentioned in previous chapters, having a well thought out, target-specific resume is essential in today's job market.

A well thought-out cover letter that sells you as an asset to the company is important.

Dressing to impress should not be just on dates. What you wear can tell a person a lot about you as a person.

Be prepared for the interview. Know how much you would like to be paid and know about the company you are applying to. Also, don't forget that negativity in any form will quickly get your resume placed in the bottom of the pile.

Now, I wanted to briefly touch on a new

hiring method that may have already affected your ability to land the job you want.

You may have already discovered that many larger companies are starting to use third party companies to run personality assessments. These assessments can be found on the companies hiring website portal or can be an in-house assessment depending on the size of the company and the position you are applying to.

The challenge with these assessments are that because there is no right or wrong answers many people find that they are trying to use methods in order to "trick" the test to make them seem more like the ideal candidate.

The problem with this tactic is that there are many factors that are being considered. When taking these assessments it would actually be in your best interest to simply answer the questions as honestly as possible.

Some examples of what may be looked at during one of these assessments. Some assessments can test how long it takes for you to answer each question.

Some assessments note when you have changed an answer.

Some assessments are designed to cause you to be under stress so it can measure your stress levels and your ability to work under pressure.

There are a few large retails chains that currently use the online assessment as part of the application process. In order to be even considered for an interview you would have to pass the assessment.

My advice to you is to avoid using too many strong responses unless you truly do feel strongly about the subject matter.

When you first read the question go with your gut instinct. These assessments are really designed to keep out undesirable employees like those who would steal from the company they work for, or those who would not be productive.
If this is not you, I have good news; you have nothing to be concerned about.

At the end of the day, your instinct will tell you what answers to put and as long as you are honest with yourself you are going to do great.

Be proud of yourself, you have taken a huge step in the right direction and you are well on your way to landing the job you want.

When the interview is done and the thank you note has been sent, you can pat yourself on the back for a job well done. If for some reason you don't land that job, don't get discouraged. You will find the right job for you. It is only a matter of time and fine tuning your skills.

A good way to prepare for your next interview is to have a friend interview you. Your friend can ask you some questions and you can answer them. Ask them to check your body language, your wording and give you advice on what to improve.

It won't happen overnight but it can happen very quickly. You just have to believe in yourself and know your worth. The moment you start to doubt yourself, you have already failed.
Keep a positive perspective and know that you are the person that they are looking for and that you will land the job you want.

You have all the tools you need to be great.

Here is to your success!

Jennifer